FORCES & MAGNETS
Let's Investigate

by Ruth Owen and Victoria Dobney

Consultant:
Nicky Waller

RUBY TUESDAY BOOKS

Published in 2021 by Ruby Tuesday Books Ltd.

Copyright © 2021 Ruby Tuesday Books Ltd.

All rights reserved. No part of this publication may be reproduced in whole or in part, stored in any retrieval system, or transmitted in any form or by any means, electronic, mechanical, photocopying, recording, or otherwise, without written permission from the publisher.

Editor: Mark J. Sachner
Designers: Emma Randall and Tammy West
Production: John Lingham

Photo credits:
Alamy: 7 (top left), 8 (bottom), 10 (bottom), 20 (top left), 27 (center), 27 (bottom); Creative Commons: 11 (top), 13 (top right), 13 (bottom); ESA: 13 (center), 24 (bottom); FLPA: 9 (top right); Getty Images: 26 (top); NASA: 14 (bottom), 16 (bottom), 17; Ruby Tuesday Books: 25 (bottom), 26 (bottom); Science Photo Library: 19 (top center); Shutterstock: Cover, 1, 2—3, 4—5, 6, 7 (top right), 7 (bottom), 8 (top), 9 (top left), 9 (bottom), 10 (top), 11 (bottom), 12, 13 (top left), 14 (top), 15 (top), 18, 19 (top left), 19 (center), 19 (bottom), 20 (top right), 20 (bottom), 21, 22 (right), 23, 24 (top), 25 (top), 27 (top), 28—29; Superstock: 16 (top), 22 (top left).

Library of Congress Control Number: 2020946810
Print (hardback) ISBN 978-1-78856-189-1
Print (paperback) ISBN 978-1-78856-190-7
eBook ISBN 978-1-78856-191-4

Printed and published in the United States of America

For further information including rights and permissions requests, please contact: shan@rubytuesdaybooks.com

www.rubytuesdaybooks.com

Contents

May the Force Be with You 4
Machines for More Force 6
All About Friction 8
Air and Water Resistance 10
What Is Gravity? 12
Falling 14
Gravity vs Air Resistance 16
Magnetic Force 18
Magnetism in Action 20
Marvelous Magnets 22
The Biggest Magnet of All 24
Magnets at Work 26
High-Speed Maglev Trains 28
Glossary 30
Index 32

The download button shows there are free worksheets or other resources available. Go to:
www.rubytuesdaybooks.com

May the Force Be with You

There are **forces** all around us. We can't see or touch forces, but we can often see what they do.

Open the refrigerator door to grab a drink. You just used a pull force.

Bump the door to close it again with your elbow—that's a push force.

How come the refrigerator door shuts tight as if it's being pulled by something invisible? That's because **magnets** inside the refrigerator and the door are exerting a magnetic force.

The bumpy soles of your sneakers create a force called **friction** that keeps your feet from sliding on slippery surfaces.

And no matter how powerful a push your legs give to launch you high into the air, a force called **gravity** will always pull you back down toward the trampoline or gymnastics mat.

Let's Talk!

Which of the forces in these three pictures are pushes, and which are pulls?
(The answer is on page 32.)

Forces in Action

When a force is exerted, or applied, to an object, what does it do?

It can change the object's **shape**.

It can change the object's **speed**.

It can change the object's **direction of movement**.

5

Machines for More Force

A small amount of force from a push or pull can be made more powerful by using simple machines such as levers, pulleys, and gears.

Levers can be used to turn a small force into a much bigger force.

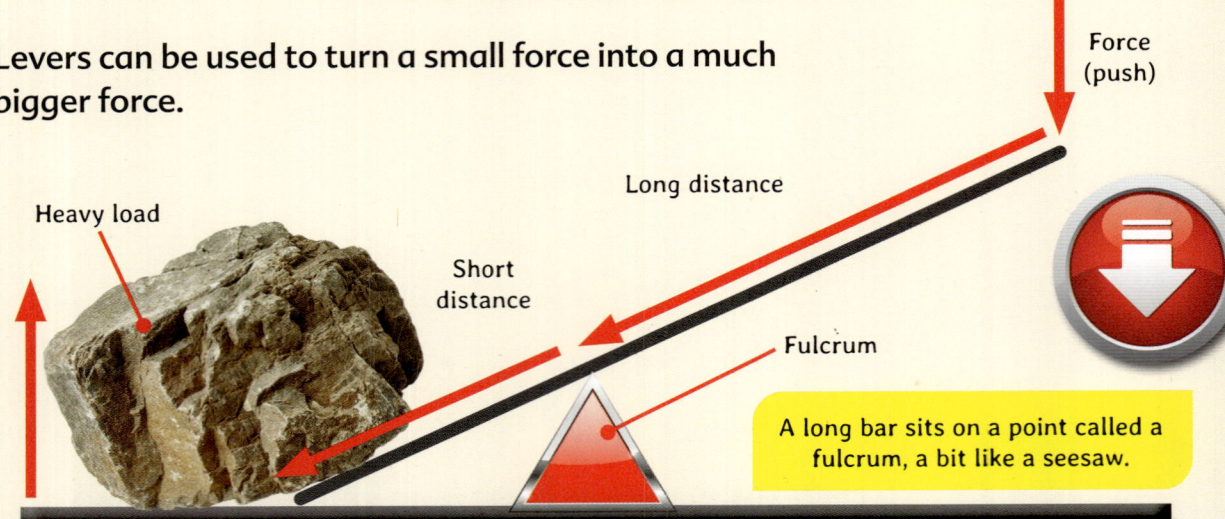

Heavy load • Long distance • Short distance • Fulcrum • Force (push)

A long bar sits on a point called a fulcrum, a bit like a seesaw.

When a small push is applied over a long distance (from a heavy load), the lever makes the job easier by converting the push into a large force over a short distance.

The lid of this paint can (the load) is difficult to lift. However, the job becomes easy with force applied by a screwdriver (the lever).

You couldn't crush this hard-shelled walnut in your hand. But this nutcracker (simple machine) is a type of lever that converts a small force from your hand into a larger crushing force.

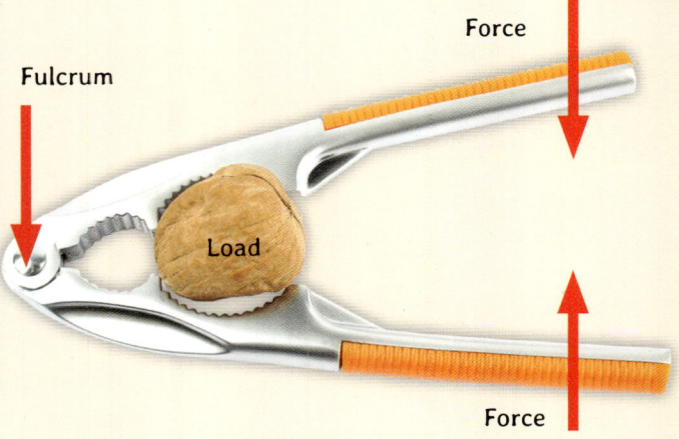

Fulcrum • Load • Force • Force

6

A pulley is a wheel with a rope wrapped around it. This simple machine changes the direction of a pull force and makes it more powerful.

If you stood up here and pulled up on the rope, it would be very difficult to lift the heavy load.

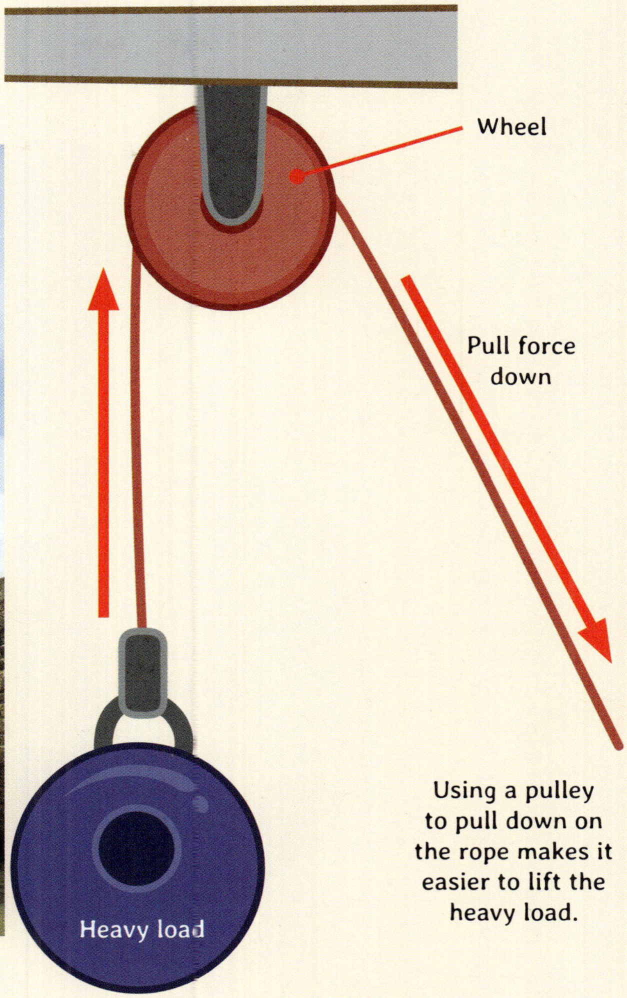

Wheel

Pull force down

Cranes use ropes and pulleys to make lifting heavy loads easier.

Heavy load

Using a pulley to pull down on the rope makes it easier to lift the heavy load.

A gear is a wheel with teeth that rotates on an axle. If gears are of different sizes, they can be used to increase the power of a turning force.

When the teeth of two gears are interlocked, gears can be used to increase speed. Gear A has 64 teeth, and Gear B has 32. By the time Gear A has rotated once, it will have rotated Gear B two times. Gear B's speed has doubled without needing twice the force.

Gears can also be used to increase force. You can use the smaller Gear B, which rotates more quickly with a small force, to turn the bigger Gear A, which will rotate more slowly but with a greater force.

A gear can change the direction of another gear. When Gear A turns clockwise, it pushes against Gear B, making it turn counterclockwise.

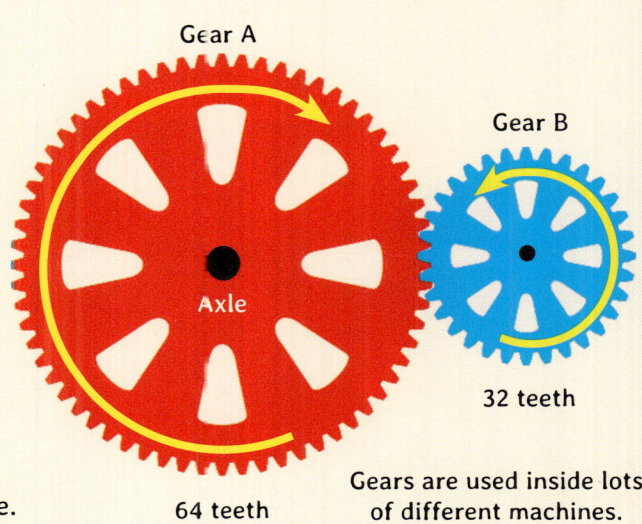

Gear A

Gear B

Axle

64 teeth

32 teeth

Gears are used inside lots of different machines.

7

All About Friction

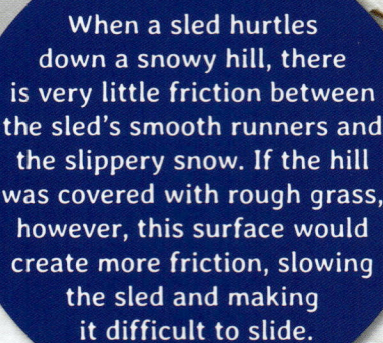

Friction is a force that is created when two surfaces rub together. The rougher the surfaces, the more friction is produced.

When a sled hurtles down a snowy hill, there is very little friction between the sled's smooth runners and the slippery snow. If the hill was covered with rough grass, however, this surface would create more friction, slowing the sled and making it difficult to slide.

Friction Heats Things Up

Have you ever seen smoke coming from the tires of a racing car as it brakes? The friction between the tires and the racetrack is producing so much heat that the tires start to smoke. Try this for yourself by rubbing your hands together hard. Can you feel the heat created by the friction between your hands?

Friction makes it more difficult for things to move and always slows a moving object down.

Frictional forces can be helpful. Friction between our shoes and a shiny floor keeps us from slipping. And friction between a car's tires and the road keeps it from skidding.

Brakes Use Friction

We use friction to slow down and stop when we're riding a bike. The bike's brakes push against the wheel, and friction between the brake and the wheel keeps it from turning.

Brake pushing against wheel

Bears Use Friction

Polar bears spend most of their time walking on ice and snow. To create friction on their dinner plate-sized paws, there are small bumps called papillae. The rough bumps help the bear's feet grip the slippery ice.

Tufts of fur between the pads and toes on a polar bear's feet also help create friction.

Rough papillae

Let's Investigate

How much friction do objects experience on ice?

Method:

1. Pour water into the tray up to a depth of about half an inch (1 cm). Carefully place the tray in the freezer so the water freezes. Make sure the tray is level.

2. Draw out a chart to record your predictions and results. Examine each object and record your predictions. Will the object:
   - Not slide?
   - Slide a little?
   - Slide a lot?

3. One at a time, place an object on the ice at one end of the tray and gently push it with your finger. Record your results.

Equipment:
- Large plastic tray with raised sides
- Water
- Paper and a pen
- Your choice of objects for testing— for example: a bottle top, a marble, a small square of cardboard, a piece of tree bark, a rock, a square of felt

	Prediction			Results		
	Not slide	Slide a little	Slide a lot	Not slide	Slide a little	Slide a lot
Bottle top		✓		Bottle top			
Marble			✓	Marble			
Cardboard				Cardboard			
Bark				Bark			
Rock				Rock			
Felt				Felt			

What is your conclusion? Complete these statements.

Items that have …………… surfaces create …………… friction and ……………

Items that have …………… surfaces create …………… friction and ……………

Air and Water Resistance

A kingfisher diving into a lake to catch fish

Friction doesn't only occur when two solid objects or surfaces move, or rub, against each other. There is also friction when objects move through air or water.

As a plane or bird flies through the air, it has to push all the air in front of it out of the way. This type of friction between an object and the air is called **air resistance**.

The shape of this kingfisher is **aerodynamic**, just like the shape of a plane. It is designed to cut through air and reduce drag, or air resistance.

Fighting Friction to Go Faster

Racing cyclists are always battling against air resistance to go that little bit faster. However, the human body is not designed to efficiently slice through air, so cyclists wear smooth suits and helmets with a **streamlined** shape. They also crouch down low over the bike's handlebars to reduce air resistance.

Just a fraction of a second faster could mean the difference between a gold and a silver medal!

Racing cyclists sometimes practice in a tunnel-like machine called a wind tunnel. As they cycle into the wind, computers calculate exactly the best position for them to use in order to reduce friction between their body and the air during a race.

10

Faster Than Sound

The Bloodhound LSR car is being designed to travel faster than sound at a record-breaking 1,000 miles per hour (1,600 km per hour). It is powered by a rocket attached to a fighter jet engine. Its long, streamlined shape will help it slice through air with a minimum amount of friction to travel half a mile (1 km) in about three seconds!

LSR stands for Land Speed Record. This is the record for the highest speed achieved by a person using a vehicle on land. As of summer 2019, the record is 763 mph (1,228 km/h).

Bloodhound LSR

Streamlined for Swimming

When you're swimming, the water must flow around you. This resistance between your body and the water slows you down. That's why dolphins, sharks, and other animals that live in water have a smooth, streamlined shape. It reduces the **water resistance**, or friction, and allows them to push through water more easily and swim faster.

What Is Gravity?

When your melting ice cream slides out of the cone and heads for the pavement, that's our next force at work—gravity!

It's gravity that makes things that are unsupported fall to the ground.

Every minute of the day, gravity is pulling you and everything around you downward toward the Earth.

When you get to the top of a giant hill on a roller coaster, it's gravity that causes your car to hurtle into a stomach-churning dive.

The Discovery of Gravity

Sir Isaac Newton was a British scientist and mathematician who was born in the 1600s. One of his most famous achievements was the discovery of gravity. Newton told people that he made his discovery while sitting in the garden watching an apple fall from a tree. He began to question why an apple always falls down from the tree and doesn't float upward or sideways. Newton realized that there was an invisible force pulling the apple and everything else on Earth down to the ground. Gravity!

Sir Isaac Newton

Inside a spacecraft or the International Space Station (ISS), astronauts are not pulled down to the ground. Instead, they float around and feel weightless.

Astronauts experience weightlessness because of the way that a spacecraft or space station moves through space. People often call this effect zero gravity.

Floating in Space

To prepare for weightlessness in space, trainee astronauts take training flights on a specially fitted aircraft nicknamed the "Vomit Comet." During a flight, the plane makes extreme climbs and dips. This creates zero gravity inside the plane for up to 25 seconds at a time. During the periods of weightlessness, the astronauts practice moving around and carrying out the tasks they will have to do in space.

Astronaut Samantha Cristoforetti tries using a drill while floating on the "Vomit Comet."

The "Vomit Comet" gets its name because the flight can make people sick.

Falling

No matter how heavy or light two objects are, gravity will always make them fall to the ground at the same speed. True?

Yes! But sometimes air resistance keeps one object from falling as quickly as another.

For example, if you drop a bowling ball and a feather, gravity will make them drop at the same speed. But the feather's shape will start to create more friction with the air, and it will float down more slowly.

The smooth bowling ball will always win the race to the ground. But what if there is no air resistance?

Scientists wanted to test this idea, so they carried out an experiment in a **vacuum**. A vacuum is a space from which all the air has been pumped.

Inside the giant airless chamber, they dropped a bowling ball and some feathers from the ceiling. Amazingly, the heavy ball and light feathers fell at exactly the same speed and hit the ground at exactly the same moment.

This experiment shows that when there is no air resistance, gravity makes all objects fall toward Earth at the same speed.

The test was carried out in NASA's 121-foot- (37-m-) high vacuum chamber in Cleveland, Ohio.

The vacuum is usually used to test how spacecraft will function in outer space, where there is no air.

Gravity Is Everywhere

Gravity doesn't only affect objects here on Earth. Earth's gravity also pulls on the Moon, keeping it orbiting, or circling around, Earth. And even from 93 million miles (150 million km) away, the Sun's gravity is pulling on Earth. Our planet, the Moon, and all the other planets in the solar system constantly orbit the Sun because we are being pulled by the Sun's gravity.

This diagram shows how gravity keeps the Moon orbiting Earth and Earth orbiting the Sun. The sizes of the objects and the distances between them are not true to life.

Just as Earth's gravity keeps you from floating up into the sky, Earth's gravity keeps the Moon from spinning off into outer space.

Let's Investigate

Gravity in Action

The size of an object's surface area affects how it pushes through the air as it falls. Let's investigate how objects of different weights and surface areas fall to the ground.

Equipment:
- A sheet of printer paper
- A sheet of printer paper squeezed into a ball
- A large pebble
- A tennis ball
- A marble
- A feather
  (Or your own choice of objects)
- A partner
- A notebook and pen

Method:

1. In your notebook, make a list of pairs of objects with different surface areas for testing. For example:
   - Pebble/feather
   - Pebble/ball of paper
   - Marble/tennis ball
   - Sheet of paper/feather

   Make up some combinations of your own, too.

2. Predict what will happen for each pair when the objects are dropped from the same height. For example, will they hit the ground at the same time, or will one object fall more slowly due to air resistance?

3. Ask your partner to hold a pair of objects, one item in each hand at arm's length. When you give the instruction, your partner must drop the objects at exactly the same time.

4. Record what happens.

Did your predictions match what happened?

How does surface area affect how quickly or slowly an object falls?

Gravity vs Air Resistance

When a sky diver jumps from a plane, gravity immediately starts pulling them toward the Earth at around 120 mph (190 km/h).

Once a sky diver opens their parachute, the size of the parachute and the air resistance against it gradually slow their descent to a more gentle and safe 30 mph (50 km/h).

Sky divers freefalling before opening their parachutes

When NASA engineers landed the robot rover *Curiosity* on Mars, they had to design a parachute to slow down a spacecraft that was carrying a heavy robot and descending at 13,000 mph (20,900 km/h)!

NASA engineers built this prototype, or test version, of *Curiosity*'s giant parachute.

Curiosity weighs 2,000 pounds (907 kilograms).

Meet Curiosity

Curiosity is fitted with a range of scientific instruments to help it study the surface of Mars. It also has a camera so it can take selfies to send back to its engineers on Earth.

On August 5, 2012, a team of engineers called the EDL (Entry, Descent, and Landing) team waited in mission control to learn if their ideas and designs had worked.

Inside its spacecraft, called an aeroshell, *Curiosity* had traveled millions of miles. Now the final minutes of its journey had arrived.

Aeroshell spacecraft

Heat shield

The aeroshell's heat shield protected the craft from the scorching heat of Mars's **atmosphere**.

Welcome to Mars

Once the aeroshell spacecraft was close to the surface of Mars, the craft's heat shield fell away. Then a descent-stage craft and rocket-powered sky crane emerged from the spacecraft to gently lower the large, heavy robot onto the rocky, dusty surface of Mars.

The aeroshell plunged into Mars's atmosphere. Then the giant parachute was successfully deployed, slowing the spacecraft to a speed of about 200 mph (320 km/h).

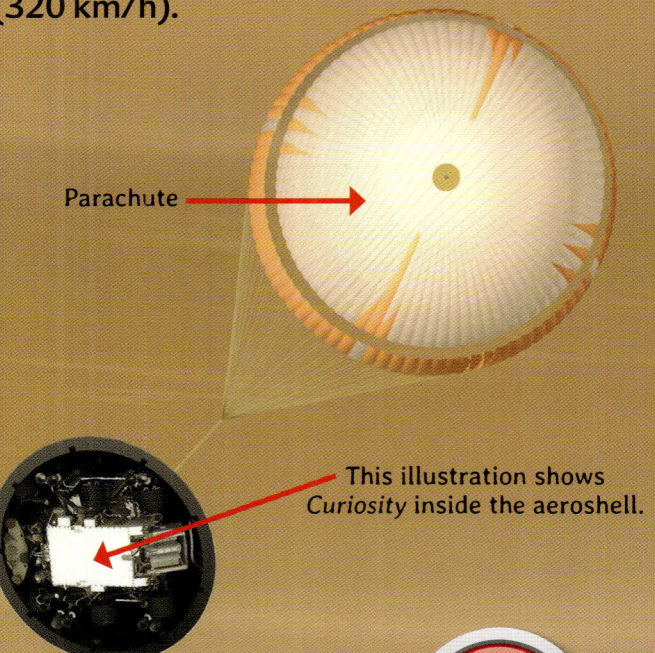

Parachute

This illustration shows *Curiosity* inside the aeroshell.

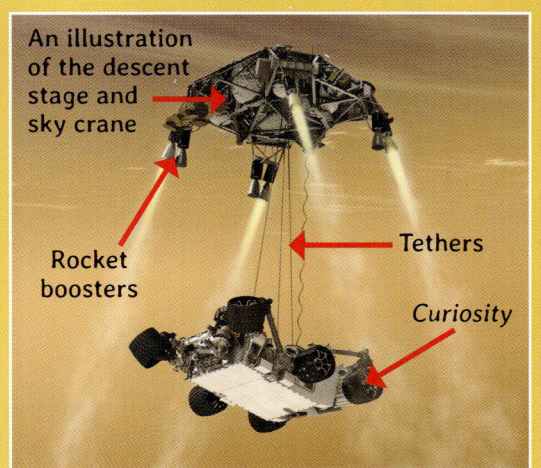

An illustration of the descent stage and sky crane

Rocket boosters

Tethers

Curiosity

Thanks to the skill of the EDL team and their understanding of gravity and air resistance, *Curiosity* the robot rover and all its onboard equipment landed safely.

17

Magnetic Force

Most forces need contact to happen between objects or substances in order for them to have an effect. But magnetic force can move objects without even touching them!

To see magnetic force in action, we use magnets. A magnet is a solid piece of metal, usually iron or steel, that is able to pull and push some other objects and other magnets.

All magnets have two ends called poles where their magnetic force is strongest.

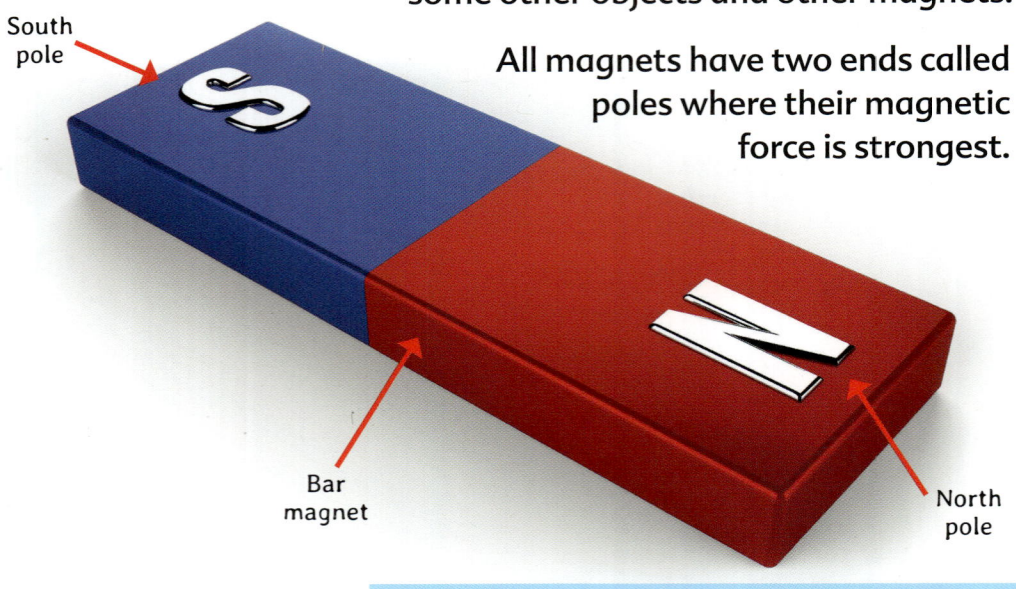

South pole

Bar magnet

North pole

Let's Test It

Tie a piece of cotton about 1 foot (30 cm) long to a paper clip. Lay the paper clip and cotton on a table. Touch a magnet to the paper clip and lift it up off the table. Take hold of the dangling cotton and pull it taut. Now gently pull the magnet away from the paper clip. The paper clip will float in mid-air, defying the force of gravity, because it is being pulled upward toward the magnet by magnetic force.

Magnets in Action

Place two bar magnets on a flat surface and try pushing them together in the ways shown in the pictures below. What do you observe and feel happening?

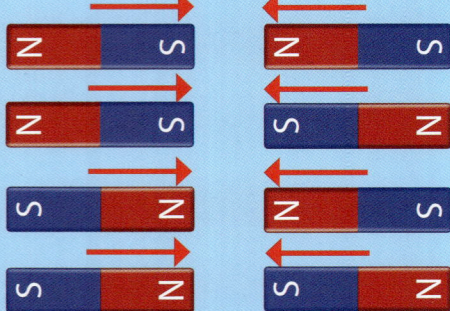

When a north pole was facing a south pole, you felt a force pulling the magnets together. But when two north poles or two south poles were facing each other, you felt a force pushing them apart.

Opposite poles of two magnets pull together, or attract. Similar poles of two magnets push apart, or repel.

Magnets come in different shapes and sizes.

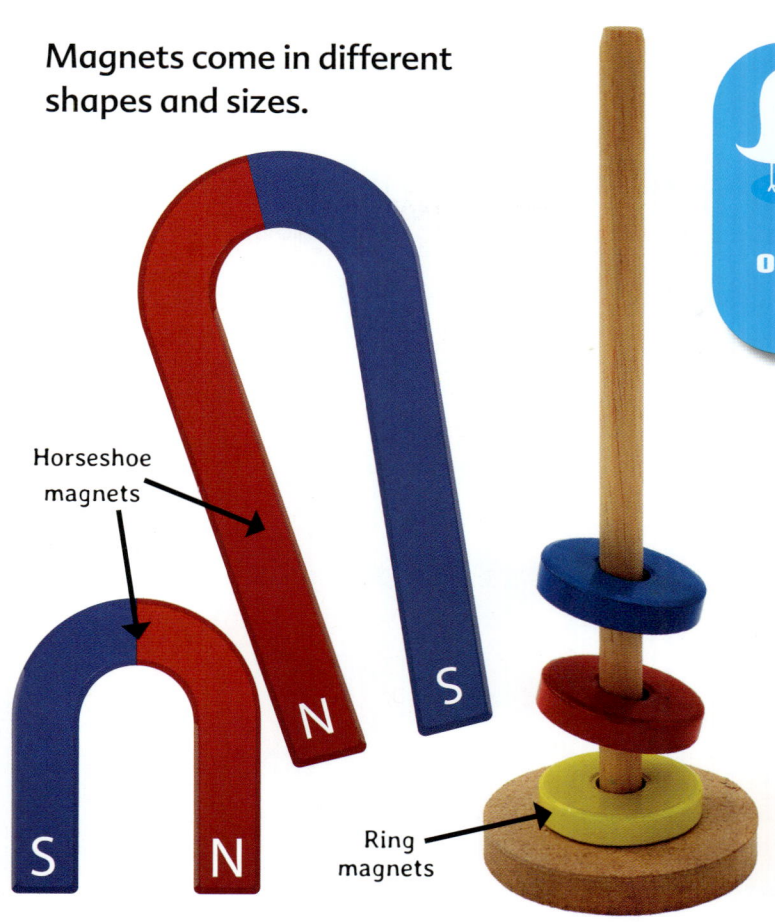

Horseshoe magnets

Ring magnets

Let's Talk!

The red and blue ring magnets on the wooden pole are not fixed. What is holding them in place?

Magnetic Cat Doors

On a magnetic cat flap, a magnet at the bottom of the flap acts like a lock. A second magnet on the cat's collar acts a little like a key. When the cat comes home, the magnet on its collar comes in contact with the magnet on the flap, and the lock opens. If a different cat tries to push open the flap, the magnetic lock stays tightly closed.

The attraction between two magnets makes them very useful in our everyday lives. Magnets are used to attach notes to refrigerator doors.

Kitchen cupboards, refrigerators, and freezers close tight because of magnets.

Magnets are also used as fasteners on backpacks, wallets, and notebooks.

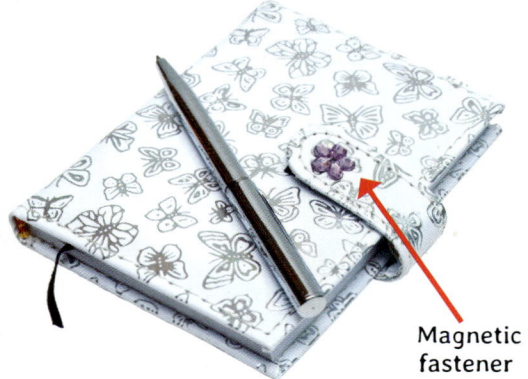

Magnetic fastener

⚠ WARNING

Computers, tablets, mobile phones, CDs, DVDs, and credit and debit cards all have magnets inside them that store data, or information. Never put another magnet close to these items, as it can cause damage to the stored data. Some people have small electronic devices called pacemakers in their chests to help their hearts beat regularly. Magnets should never be put near the chest of a person with a pacemaker. You should never put small magnets in or near your mouth, as you could swallow them.

Magnetism in Action

The invisible area around a magnet that attracts or repels some other objects and magnets is called a **magnetic field**.

These magnets have been sprinkled with tiny pieces of metal called iron filings that are attracted to the magnets.

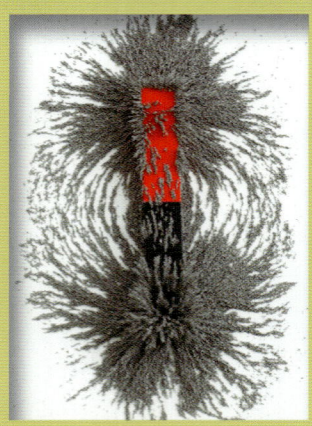

Where do you think the magnetic field is strongest on each magnet?

Let's Investigate

Every magnet produces a different-sized magnetic field around itself. The more powerful a magnet is, the larger its magnetic field will be. Let's investigate!

How large is my magnet's magnetic field?

Equipment:
- A ruler
- A paper clip
- A bar magnet
- A notebook and pencil

Method:

① Put the ruler on a table and place a paper clip alongside one end. The paper clip should line up with zero on the ruler. Place your magnet at the other end of the ruler.

② Hold the ruler in place and with the other hand slowly slide the magnet toward the paper clip. The moment the paper clip moves, stop moving the magnet. Record where on the ruler you stopped the magnet. Now repeat with the other pole and record your result.

③ Next, place just one of the magnet's poles against the ruler. Line up the paper clip with zero in the position shown below. Push the magnet toward the paper clip. When the paper clip moves, stop moving the magnet and record the measurement. Repeat with the other pole in this position.

④ Place your magnet on your notebook and draw around it. Then use your results to draw its magnetic field.

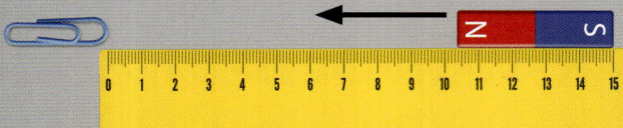

Ancient Magnets

The magnets we are using for the investigations in this book are made of metal and were **magnetized** in a factory. But magnets also form in nature. Around 2,600 years ago, the ancient Greeks discovered that pieces of rock that they called lodestones attracted iron and acted as magnets. The lodestones were made from a type of naturally magnetized rock called magnetite.

Magnetite rock

No one knows for sure, but the name "magnet" may have come from lodestones found in a part of ancient Greece called Magnesia. Today this area is part of modern-day Turkey.

Imagine you are a person living in ancient times and you find a piece of rock that's a magnet. What would you use your discovery to do?

Let's Investigate

What kinds of materials are attracted to magnets?

Equipment:
- A magnet
- Objects for testing
- A notebook and pen

Brass key   Aluminum can   Foil   Gold ring

Method:

❶ Look at the objects in the pictures.

Which objects do you think will be attracted to a magnet?

❷ Record your predictions and then go on a magnet hunt to find as many of these objects as possible. Touch the magnet to each one and observe if it is attracted. Record your results.

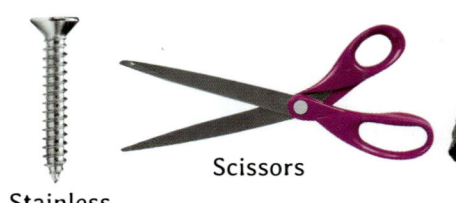 

Stainless steel screw   Scissors   Rock

Did your predictions match what happened?

What is your conclusion? Which kinds of materials are attracted to a magnet?

Silver earring   Eraser   Wood

Marvelous Magnets

Magnets are only attracted to some metals. Not all kinds of metals are magnetic.

Iron and steel (which is a mixture of iron and carbon) are both magnetic. Metals such as aluminum, brass, silver, and gold are not attracted to magnets.

A piece of plastic on its own is not attracted to a magnet. But if a magnet is held to a plastic-covered metal object, such as a stainless steel paper clip or thumbtack, the magnet's magnetism still works through the plastic.

Let's Investigate

Can a magnet's magnetic field be blocked?

Equipment:
- A magnet
- 5 paper clips
- Materials for testing: a plastic container (such as an empty butter or cream cheese container), cardboard, a small, flat glass dish, a plastic plate, styrofoam, felt, a glass of water
- A notebook and pen

Method:

1. To prepare for your investigation, pour about 0.25 inch (0.5 cm) of water into a plastic container and freeze it.

2. Look at the materials for testing.

Do you think they can block a magnetic field? Record your predictions.

3. Begin by placing the paper clips on the cardboard. Hold a magnet under the cardboard and try to move the clips. Repeat with the glass dish, plastic plate, styrofoam and felt.

4. Put the paper clips into the glass of water. Try to make the paper clips move by placing the magnet on the outside of the glass. Record your results.

5. Take the container of ice you prepared from the freezer. Place the paper clips on the ice. Hold a magnet under the container and try to make the paper clips skate across the ice.

Did your results match your predictions? Which materials can block a magnet's magnetic field?

It's possible for a magnet to pass on its magnetism to another metal object.

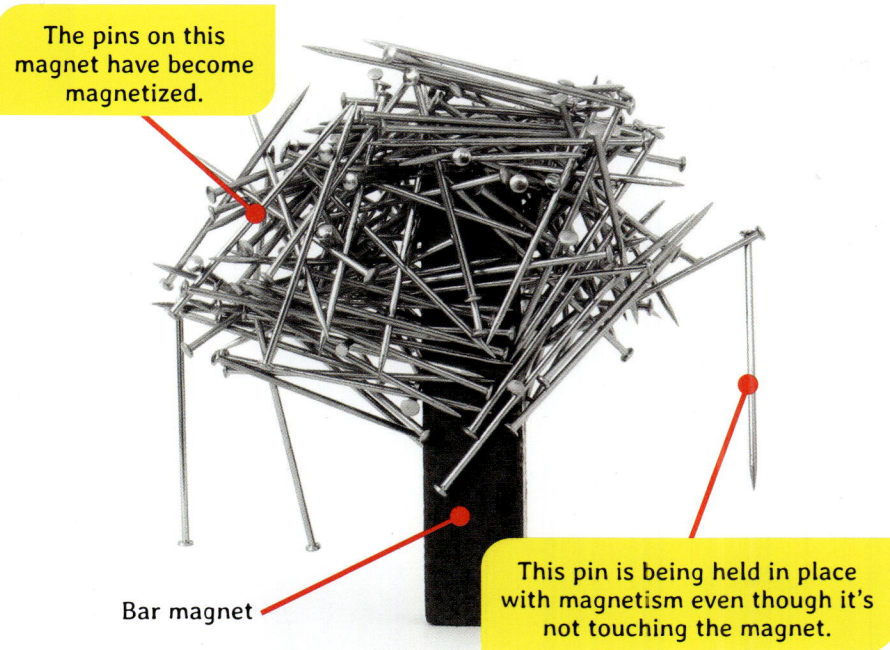

The pins on this magnet have become magnetized.

Bar magnet

This pin is being held in place with magnetism even though it's not touching the magnet.

Let's Test It

Try magnetizing an object made of steel, such as a spoon, screw, or pair of scissors. Begin by checking that the object you've chosen is attracted to your magnet. Next, rub the magnet against the object for about a minute to magnetize it. Now place a metal paper clip onto your magnetized object to discover if there is attraction. You've just made a magnet!

Let's Investigate

How strong is my magnet?

Test the strength of a magnet by discovering how many objects it can attract.

Equipment:
- 3 magnets of different sizes
- Handful of paper clips
- A helper
- A notebook and pen

Method:

① Ask your helper to hold a magnet. Place a paper clip to one of the magnet's poles so it slightly overhangs.

② Now touch a second paper clip to the first.

Is the second paper clip attracted to the first? What does this tell us about magnetism?

③ Keep adding paper clips to make the longest chain possible.

How many paper clips could you add before the magnetism of the chain became too weak? Record your results.

④ Now repeat the investigation with a different magnet.

How long a chain will this magnet support? Record your predictions and test them.

23

magnetism, turning Earth into a huge magnet with a north and south pole.

Earth's magnetism creates a vast invisible magnetic field around our planet called the **magnetosphere**.

A Protective Magnetic Field

The Sun constantly releases a stream of tiny particles called the solar wind. If our planet were not protected by the magnetosphere, the solar wind would destroy Earth's atmosphere, which protects us from harmful **radiation**. The atmosphere also stops too much heat from reaching Earth, which would dry up all the water and make life on Earth impossible.

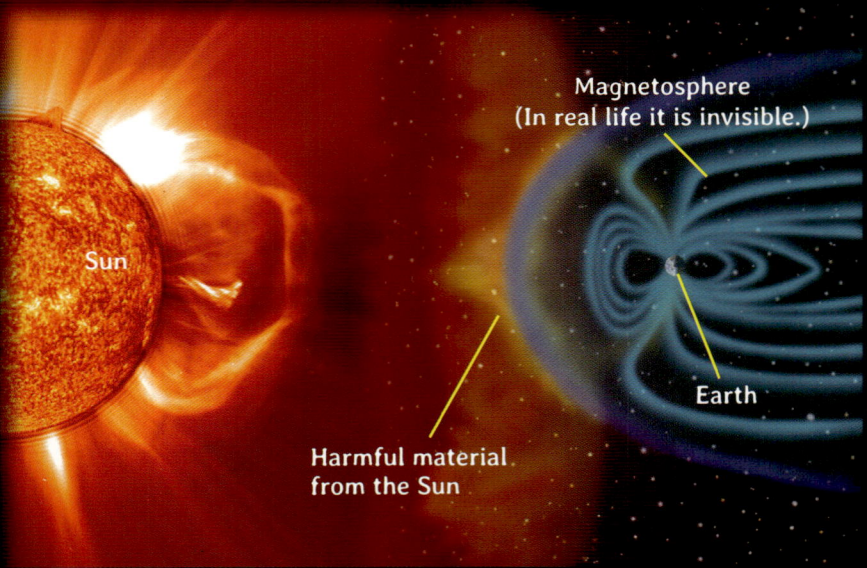

This illustration shows how Earth's magnetosphere might look. The distance between the Sun and Earth is not true to life.

Earth's magnetism allows us to find out which direction we are traveling in by using a **compass**—even if we are out at sea or in the middle of a thick forest.

The needle in a compass is always pulled to the north by Earth's magnetism. This allows you to know which way is north.

Needle pointing north

Compass

Why do magnets have a north and south pole? If you hold up a bar magnet by a string tied around its middle, it will always turn and **align** its north and south poles to Earth's magnetic north and south poles.

Let's Make It

It's possible to make your own compass with water and a sewing needle. In fact, if you have a needle and you're in a forest, you can make a compass with a leaf and a puddle!

Equipment:
- A needle
- A bar magnet
- A leaf
- Water, such as a puddle

Method:

1. Place the needle on the magnet so its point is facing toward the magnet's south pole. Leave overnight, and the needle will become magnetized.

2. Float the leaf on the puddle. Gently place the needle onto the leaf. Now that the needle is floating on water, it can move freely.

3. Watch the needle. Earth's magnetism will pull the point of the needle toward north.

4. To be sure your leaf and needle compass is working, test it by gently moving the leaf with your finger so the needle is pointing in a different direction. The leaf and needle will turn so that the needle's point is once again pointing north.

Magnets at Work

In factories and at junkyards and waste recycling plants, large magnets controlled by electricity are used for lifting and sorting metals.

An **electromagnet** has a magnetic field created by electricity. The electricity is turned on when there's metal to be lifted, and off when the magnet is not being used.

Magnets for Trash Recycling

In some areas, we separate paper, plastic, glass, and metal from other trash to be taken to a waste recycling plant. These materials travel along conveyor belts and are sorted by workers and machines. In some places, an electromagnetic separator attracts pieces of metal, such as iron and steel, from the waste, lifting them from the conveyor belt. Then these metals can be recycled to make new metal.

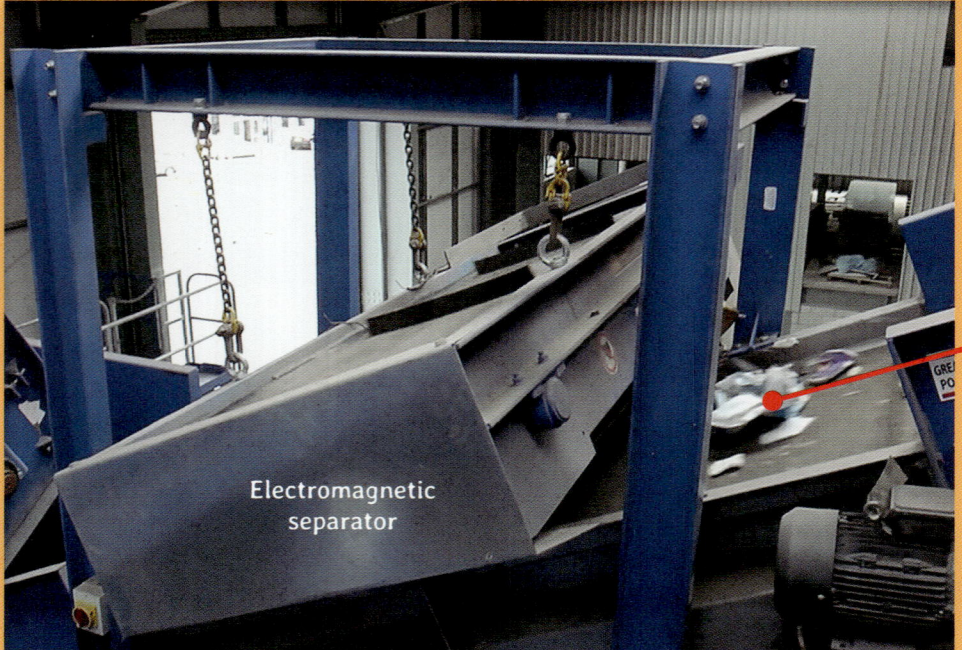

Trash on conveyor belt

Electromagnetic separator

Separating Scrap

Junkyards are places where old washing machines, refrigerators, cars, and other metal objects are collected. Iron and steel, which can be sold for recycling, are separated from other metals and materials with an electromagnetic crane.

When the electrical current is switched on, the powerful magnet attracts iron and steel objects.

Once the electricity is switched off, the magnet is no longer magnetized.

For many years, refrigerators went into **landfill** when they no longer worked. Now special recyling plants can recycle about 95 percent of the metal, plastic, and other materials in a refrigerator. Electromagnets play a big part in this process.

This photo (taken from the air by a drone) shows refrigerators waiting to be recycled. A special recycling plant may process up to 15,000 refrigerators each week.

Separating Mixed Materials

At a refrigerator recycling plant, old refrigerators go into a machine called a grinder or shredder, which chops the refrigerators into pieces that can be no longer than a grain of rice. The pieces travel along a conveyor belt and go under a large electromagnetic separator. The powerful magnet attracts all the pieces of steel and iron from the chopped-up refrigerator mixture, ready for recycling into new refrigerators and other products.

Chopped-up metal from an old refrigerator

High-Speed Maglev Trains

Imagine speeding across countries at hundreds and maybe even thousands of miles an hour. That's what the many engineers and designers who are developing Maglev trains hope may one day be possible.

Maglev trains are powered and controlled by magnets. They **levitate**, or hover, above the tracks. In tests they have reached speeds of more than 370 mph (600 km/h).

Very little noise and no harmful fumes

The Shanghai Maglev Train

No friction from wheels or the track

The name "Maglev" comes from the words *magnetic levitation*. Engineers around the world are developing, building, and testing different versions of Maglev trains.

The Shanghai Maglev Train

The only Maglev train that currently carries paying passengers is the Shanghai Maglev Train in China. It runs from Shanghai Pudong International Airport to the outskirts of Shanghai. The 19-mile (30.5-km) journey takes just eight minutes, and passengers can watch a display showing the speed!

Maglev Technology

There are two different Maglev train systems.

In one system, the magnets on the track and on the bottom of the train have similar poles facing each other. The magnets repel each other, keeping the train from touching the tracks and making it look as if it's on an invisible cushion.

The second system uses attraction between electromagnets. Magnets on the train and on the tracks have opposite (or attracting) poles facing each other. However, the magnets don't touch each other. That's because the electrical current in the magnets is switched on and off, on and off incredibly fast. The magnets try to attract but never quite make it, leaving the train hovering in the air.

Both systems also use magnets to move the levitating trains along the tracks at high speed.

Supersonic Trains

With no friction on the tracks, the only force that stops a Maglev train from going faster and faster is air resistance. Scientists estimate that if a Maglev train could be placed in a vacuum tube with no air resistance, speeds of more than 2,100 mph (3,500 km/h) could be possible. This is faster than the speed of sound and many times faster than passenger planes can fly. Will we one day travel on **supersonic** trains? For now, no one can say for sure!

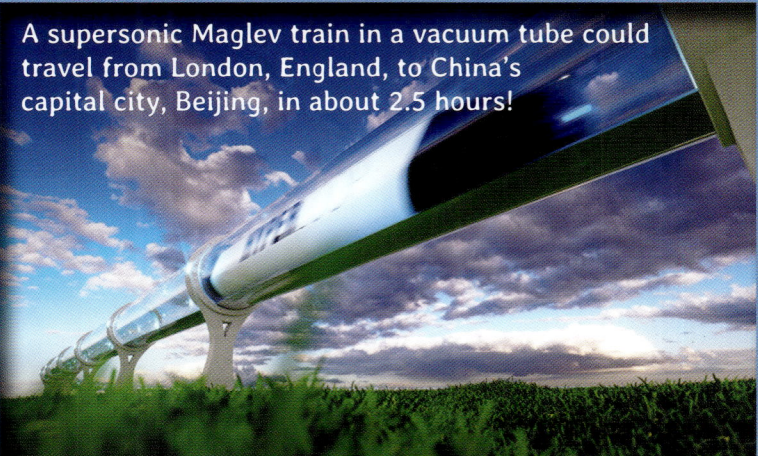

A supersonic Maglev train in a vacuum tube could travel from London, England, to China's capital city, Beijing, in about 2.5 hours!

This illustration shows how a vacuum tube might look.

Glossary

aerodynamic
Having a pointed, smooth shape that reduces air resistance, or drag. Planes and birds have aerodynamic shapes.

air resistance
A type of friction between an object and the air that makes it harder for the object to move through the air.

align
To line up or point toward.

atmosphere
A layer of gases surrounding a planet, moon, or star.

attract
To pull toward—for example, a magnet attracts iron and steel.

compass
A device that a person can use to check their direction of travel. Compasses have needles that always point north because of Earth's magnetism.

electromagnet
A magnet with a magnetic field that is produced by an electric current. An electromagnet's magnetism can be turned on and off.

exert
To apply or put effort into use—for example, a gear exerts a force on the gear next to it.

force
A push or a pull—for example, friction is a force that pushes against an object to slow it down, and gravity is a force that pulls unsupported objects on Earth down toward the ground.

friction
A force that pushes against an object to slow it down.

gravity
The force that pulls things together; on Earth, gravity pulls everything down toward the ground.

landfill
A place where a large quantity of trash is buried in the ground to get rid of it.

levitate
To rise up and hover in the air.

magnet
A piece of metal (usually iron) that is magnetized, which means it attracts some other metals, such as iron and steel.

magnetic field
The invisible area around a magnet that attracts or repels some metals and other magnets.

magnetic force
The force from a magnet that attracts some metals; also the force that attracts or repels other magnets.

magnetized
Having a magnetic field that can attract and repel.

magnetosphere
The protective magnetic field surrounding Earth. Earth's magnetism is produced by the movement of Earth's core.

molten
Turned to liquid by heat.

radiation
Energy that is radiated (released) in waves or particles, such as light energy from the Sun. Some forms of radiation can be harmful.

repel
To push away—for example, the similar poles of two magnets repel each other.

streamlined
Having a shape that gives very little resistance to air or water.

supersonic
Having a speed that is faster than sound. Sound travels at 1,125 feet (343 m) per second.

vacuum
A space that contains absolutely nothing—not even air.

water resistance
A type of friction between an object and water that makes it harder for the object to move through the water.

Index

A
air resistance 10—11, 14—15, 16—17, 29
animals 9, 10—11, 19
astronauts 13

B
bicycles 9, 10
Bloodhound LSR car 11
brakes 8—9

C
compasses 25
core (of Earth) 24
Cristoforetti, Samantha 13
Curiosity robot 16—17

E
electromagnets 26—27, 29

F
friction 4, 8—9, 10—11, 14, 28—29

G
gears 6—7
gravity 5, 12—13, 14—15, 16—17, 18

I
International Space Station (ISS) 13

L
Land Speed Record 11
levers 6

M
Maglev trains 28—29
magnetic fields 20, 22, 24, 26
magnetite 21
magnetosphere 24
magnets 4, 18—19, 20—21, 22—23, 24—25, 26—27, 28—29
Moon, the 15

N
Newton, Sir Isaac 13

P
parachutes 16—17
pull forces 4—5, 6—7, 12—13, 15, 16, 18, 25
pulleys 6—7
push forces 4—5, 6—7, 9, 10—11, 15, 18—19

R
recycling 26—27
roller coasters 12

S
Shanghai Maglev train 28—29
simple machines 6—7
sky divers 16
Sun, the 15, 24
supersonic trains 29

V
vacuums 14, 29
"Vomit Comet" 13

W
water resistance 10—11
weightlessness (in space) 13

Answers

Page 5:
A push force changes the yellow ball's shape. A pull by the dog walker slows down the dogs. And a header (push) from the player changes the ball's direction.